CLOUD CATCHER

By

Roger L Tougas

© Copyright 2014, Roger L Tougas, All rights reserved. No part of this book may be reproduced, stored in a retrieval system, or transmitted by any means, electronic, mechanical, photocopying, recording, or otherwise, without written permission from the author.

Quotations

"Imagine all the people living life for free."

John Lennon

*"What is it like to live in a society
with shackles on your hands?"*

Bob Dylan

"Could you be loved and be loved?"

Bob Marley

*"Are you a little black rain cloud
or a moonlit masquerade?"*

Roger Tougas

Table of Contents

The Poem...7
A Sordid Misery..8
The Iceman Com'meth..11
Could It Be?..13
Willow Will You Weep For Me?..15
I Let A Song Go..18
A Tulip Wedding..19
Falling Up..20
Tabasco For My Eyes..21
Hummingbird..22
Bog Beast..24
World Be Free...25
A Song Of Myself..27
Sing Low...41
Sweet Favor..42
Gothic Moonrise..43
Ghost Town..44
Medusa...46
Everlasting..48
The Makeshift Paragon..50
Suspended..52
Time Square...54
Inhibitions...55
Tatters..56
Sylvia..57
Predestine Journey..59
Withering Hearts...60
Blown Glass..61
Birdsong...62
Stones..63
Luck Be A Stone Lion..64
Frenchman's Reef...65
Star Turtle..66
Pemigewasset River..67
Black Cat..68
The Ugly Waltz..69

Grammy 70
Anne..71
Venus If You Will..73
Pearl Diver..74
Secret Garden..75
Dueling Dragons 77
A Plaid Style...78
A Ruby Desire...79
New Moon Cabin 81
Don't You Weep..82
Cloud Catcher...84
Paper Moon 85
Portraits 87
Sunflower..93
Paper Tiger..94
A Pale Gray Silent Symphony...............................95
Camelot...97
Suburbia..99
Virgin Islands..101
Iceland...102
Harvest Moon..104
Landmarks...105
1968: Today is the Day.......................................106
Darfur..108
A Dry Mist Illusion...109
Haiku Corner...111

5

For my son,
"Daddy, I love you 'way up to the moon!"
Kevin, age 4

The Poem
(For Ted Hughes)

"Which one of us, in his moments of ambition, has not dreamed of the miracle of poetic prose, musical, without rhythm and without rhyme, supple enough and rugged enough to adapt itself to the lyrical impulses of the soul, the undulations of reverie, the jibes of conscience?"

    Charles Baudelaire, 19th Century

The poetic devotion is a meter ebbing
  through a bio-rhythmic life.
After all, what is, Walt Whitmans' take
  on the body electric? Is it,
  a portrayal of heart songs;
  a cast of bipolar impressions;
  an abstract expression;
  raw imagery in sharp focus;
  a lyrical showpiece;
  a toxic and timeless piece;
  a bonded cause;
  a spectacular event;
  a rotten eyesore;
  the holy grail of lore;
  an immortal faith;
  a vivid testament;
  a hieroglyphic chronicle;
  a fabled spin thrift;
  a primal urge;
  a haloed frolic;
  a splendor remembered;
  a meaning to the earthly facts
  and figures;
  a portal of dreams.

November 2003

A Sordid Misery

The solo pledge scores
a mystic wilderness sys-
tem of champions.

The sun rises sweet
on the horizon with a
dry mist illusion.

The autumn leaves drift
by my sleepless window beyond
a flint-shadow's ear.

I was the river.
I was a lunar tide pool.
I was an island

and the sea roared
like a chorus turning cheek.
The lazy straights

whispered for heavens'
evergreen gate holding on
to mortal eyes.

A cold season bleeds
through the burning embers of
blissful memories.

Suspicious mindsets
sabotage memorial
pledges to be free.

The hypnotic dance
of a death angel wanders
past sacred tears.

Her body spins past

the mortal thief's never
ending darkness and

marches over heralds
blind sin for the clockwork blue
news of tomorrow.

The birth in funeral
spirals into the terror
of madness; in shades of

grief: Jacob's ladder.
The frailty in the willow
terrifies me.

The sounds of wilderness
tickle peppermint winds on
a rose-plum atmosphere.

The lord's of sage rush
thread the needle-eye of a
mint jubilee.

I bare no grudge to
a loving hand. The sands of
time hid the pearl light.

A fist full of dollars
for the fiddler who plays
to a slow gin fizz.

A recipe for
a silk wood fantasy of sweet
and tender mercy.

I long to be in
a secret world beyond the
name who lost its pearl.

I would feel strong

and I would be laughing.
I would be laughing...

October 2005

The Iceman Com'meth
(Jefferson, NH: Jan 1996: for Sting)

Once he trekked into the
  driven snow for miles
    before he broke through.
Long shadows blended
  into the frozen tree line.

A blustery squall
  masked the sunlit
    interior.
Colossal snow drifts
  covered
    the temple mount.

The Nordic tracker's
  painstaking pace
    was suddenly halted
      in its tranquil
        mountain escape.

His skies flash freeze.
The ice cakes formed
  to splinter.
A cold sweat soaked
  through his inner layers.
A froth of foam
  adorned his exterior.

The shattered solitude was
    bone cold to any semblance
      of good cheer.
I've come to know that
  the iceman com'meth
    in a frosty glaze coverall,
and a blue cord steel interior.

The iceman com'meth

using uncharted trails with
  his face cooled to a pale gray;
he com'meth
  to a brand new day.

He com'meth more wholesome today.

February 2004

Could It Be?

(for Jack Kerouac and to those who know)

Could it be that we missed the point of our dreams?
Could it be that we dismissed our heart screams?
Could it be that we lost our way indeed?

Go on,
tell me something good;
tell it as you like it;
tell it like you should.

Could it be marble doves flying
  behind that waterfall?

Could it be that the mystic river
  harbors blue angels?

Could it be that the serpent's tongue
  has ended its run?

Could it be that we are on the upside
  of anger?

Could it be a dangerous passage?

Could it be that we ignored the echoes of the
  sweet love chime?

Go on,
tell me something good;
tell it as you like it;
tell it like you should.

Could it be that we merely hear
  a song of suspense?

Could it be the rot of community
  setting in?

Sometimes, I like to cut the silken threads
  off of my dream catcher; but I realize,

that a rainbow always contemplates
  good karma.

Come on, sing to me while I still bleed;
  tell me, now that the night fades away.

I know that, that sweet inspiration, will
  surely color my way.

Go on,
tell me something good;
tell it as you like it;
tell it like you should.

Why don't you tell me about
the olive branch of n i r v a n a?

August 2005

Willow Will You Weep For Me?

(For Langston Hughes & Wes Montgomery)

Willow will you weep for me?
In tangled dreadlocks you marshal
a melancholy tune.
The autumn breeze keeps time.

I've been everywhere
  but I've been unaware.

Big willow across the sky,
won't you help me find the time?
Helpless, helpless, helpless.

I ponder as I wander;
'cause I want my ticket to ride.
Willow, how is it that you're so calm?

The willow responds in whispers.

*I've seen what lies beneath
mankind's beliefs.*

*I've known the prairie calm
at midnight.*

*I've felt the jungle rot
on my wholesome bark.*

*I've been everywhere,
and I've been nowhere.*

*I've seen the fires
overcome by rain.*

*I've witnessed the star dust
shown bright.*

*I've seen the goldenrod tickle
a flushing meadow.*

*I've cast a long shadow in
morning glories peaceful path.*

*I've felt the sting of acid rain
on my tender canopy.*

*I've heard the echoes
of a sweet hearts' desire.*

I bear the tattoos of love slogans.

*I've seen the sands of time
bury lost lives.*

*I am reticent but maybe
you didn't know me then.*

Meanwhile

The wind trumpets a desolate tune.
Golden leaves swing in the breeze,
the swirls motion to fence me in.

Chickadees wade in on a shallow bath
wading and singing in serial lanes.
The breeze wreaks of skunk weed.

O weep, willow, weep. . .
wash away the stain of night and
summon all birds of flight

to sing a sweet song until
we have our bonanza
played out in heart songs.

The willow branches assemble
into a boars head with the

winds howling until dawn.
I shout out, *"I wonder if I'll find her!"*
The leafy wit replies: *"the dereliction of you*
is past all sweet blessings. . ."

August 2004

I Let A Song Go

(For Thelonious Monk)

I let a song go
  I touch the world

I tap around the slide bar
  I let it flow

Pride and prejudice knows
  the mother of black pearls

The rigid outcroppings scar
  in a garden of steel tulips

I let a song go
  I touch the world

I tap around the slide bar
  I let it flow

The tender skin of slumber
  a sting of acid notes

The unseen mystic rose
  finally awoke

I let a song grow
  I steal away the hour

The offerings are true
  I let them know

      March 2004

A Tulip Wedding

(Coast Guard Beach, Sept. 2004)

a Jewish wedding on a blonde beach
before the purple haze of dusk
the families' own, in love with the way,
prepare the fire pit
the earnest bride fondles her bouquet
the patient groom meditates in the salt air
the surf is brisk
a father and son running wind sprints
along the waters edge
the sand pipers are aroused
a rustic coast guard station scales the inland
tide whipped breakers mask hidden family capers
the moment surrenders itself to the Rabbi
with the ageless smile

> a tulip wedding
> in picture perfect setting
>
> two hearts as one
> mind matters undone
>
> coastal melody
> in pearl-clad rhapsody
>
> pastel tapestry
> in mosaic registry
>
> a flame red tint
> on fortunes mint

a splendor remembered one fine day
or what you will

July 2007

Falling Up
(For George Harrison)

hear the call of love's laughter
  o' how it beckons me

a sweet and tender mercy
  a rain swept flowers curtsy

a keen wit failing safe
  a saucy fellow falling up

brilliant flashes winking thunder
  from a distant shore

lost faces drifting in darkness
  trouble ripples in the moon shine

lost in the shadows and fog
  a temptation for star dust

gods eye lifts over the horizon
  the holy trinity tames the lion

the sun tower of will and might
  burning eternally bright

forever and always standing up
  forever and always falling up

January 2004

Tabasco For My Eyes

The living order is an urban
  landscape's fresh blood ore:
  a mammoth lunar tide crashing
  in a thunderous roar;
  the desert calm at twilight;
  a comet cutting the night sky; or
  a total eclipse of the sun.
Red hot natural events are
  a Tabasco for my eyes.
Great music governs my pulse.
Van Gogh's art captured the
  serenity and strive of life;
Shakespeare's works revealed
  its pain and passion.
The crimson sun kissing
  aqua marine shores.
A magnificent desolation of panoramic
  spaces surrounded by red canyon walls;
  the purple mountain majesty.
A simple orchid bloom in a
  moonlit masquerade.
The American scene taking
  a stab at me.

February 2003

Hummingbird

O hummingbird,
  O walela bird,
    what have you heard?

The harmonious bird swiftly
forages on hyped up energy
bursting at the scene.

Hummingbird central is alive
at the magnolia trees.
A coat of color in silk-like sheen;

  a fiery red,
   a golden lace,
    an emerald green;
        all glisten in streams.

A zig, a zag, a fuzzy buzz;
the needle nose beak
delicately extracts floral treats.

It levitates on cellophane wings,
never hesitating,
to take its daily intake.

In the wink of eye
the hummingbird flies by;
truly, an aerial acrobat of the skies.

Busily,
they band about the magnolia
soaking up natures candy.

O to float freely,
  to be heard,
    not often seen;

    in glossy
      c o l o r s,
         uniquely themed.

Hummingbird central,
 comes alive,
out by the magnolia grove.

         April 2003

Bog Beast

O beautiful butterfly
fly freely, away;
freely it flutters
giving way to the others;
a free flight giving way
to a lengthy stay,
out by the bog
one fine day.

A caterpillar's metamorphosis
is ogre-lye transformed
on paper wings;
a monstrous image forms,
a beast, a bog beast.
On flippable wings
a ghastly distortion appears;
emblazoned fury
 or plain foolery.

The inner secrets
of a natural defense
is hereby revealed.
Reptilian predators are fooled
by horrifying appearances;
suddenly, a reversal is sprung;
the reptilian predator
fears being digested.
The butterfly slips by
on smoke and mirrors.

No butterfly is ever defenseless.
No metamorphosis is ever finished.

Fly freely away butterfly;
live on to enjoy another fine day;
fly away, fly, fly.
April 2003

World Be Free

(For Dr. Martin Luther King Jr.)

There was a dream
  where I felt alive
mixing in with color
  with no civil strife.

The real me is made serious,
made curious, self made to see.

I see a star laced riddle
  forming into a peaceful
taxonomy. One step beyond

is a place where good themes
  are aligned to your dreams.
If I could only dream
  a little dream of need.

World be free!
            World be free!
                        World be free!

My world are words spoken
  of truth in sweet homily;
must it catch on, so slowly,
  like the growth of a tree?

What have we done
  to our friends?
A riotous path pierces
  the angel's heart song.

The pawn master orders
  blood stones to be
    thrown. What is

the endless trinity of

   peace and harmony?
One world released is
  the seed of tranquility.

I dream a little dream of free.

O please don't
  keep me waiting;
    now that your bodies gone,
    dreamer, you will *live*.

March 2003

A Song Of Myself

My life longs to keep from
a restless place revisited:
What more do I stand for?
A steeple chase turned fleet or
my place, my time to reap!
The warrior poet is off
                and running.

I pace myself;
  I stow my rage;
    I mellow easy;
  I live in a cage:
I long to be free
of any need.

My inner child races along
the limits of life's striking melodies.
A fluid flow of impressions run deep
in with attitudes glowing meek.
The bitter sweet attitude reaps.
The faint of heart gently weeps.
An ageless love offers a remedy.

O come take me home
to a place I've never known.
A place of wide open spaces
where the days pour blue with
pastel colors running through. I'll
immerse myself in its natural brew.

Big blue sky parades pour through
keyholes from America's rustic
past. Frontier dreams are kept
in a lock box at the dead poet's
society. I wanted poetry to be
in rhythm with the sea; the great
expanse, furious highs, dead calm

lows, and cleansing foams.

At the birth of our nation we had
a state of amazing grace; over time,
it fluxed into a state of grace
and grim. The ego driven duality
in the body politic has stained
our national identity. We abuse
the time honored creed: *"let he
who is without sin cast the first stone."*
I will drink blood tea over the bones
of our forefathers.

And who shall decide if one is godless?
Islam? Christians? Buddhist? Or the Jews?
Whom are they who hide behind the
house of poverty and oppression.
In the grip of a mad sorrow,
black tears spill into fear.
We will forever mingle with the
demons and their dark lies. Way
down along the edge of all reason
we can live beyond a dream.

The winter sky opens to a cozy
hospitality. A tangerine-plum vale
tickles a pale gray dusk. I fall
victim to its majestic chronicles.
The sun wheel paints our millen-
nium visions for tomorrow.
A life line extends over the
horizon touching a bright new day.

You have but a memory of me,
a fractured filament,
not to touch, save for looking;
not what is important to me.
Look at me, I sing, heartfelt;
a song of myself with a manic
chorus, in the light of a distant
shore; an ageless song to a

silent audience.

I dance in a fog of the saucy
delta blues. The moon hangs low
and large. It is hard to make sense
of big suspicions with small intentions.
O love labors' lost in the dust of
broken promises. Go on, take a load
off me sweet Gypsy, in the moon
light of the billowing blues.

The dowd grazes in sugar land but
her milk is *bittersweet*, her kids
roam aimlessly. Are they confused
about who they are and what they
should be doing? I find their bleated
sense of things annoying, go on and
learn the myth o of the world.

The flower child sees the world
through rose colored glasses.
A big sky filled with diamonds.
A lake in the clouds filled
with new born cheer;
bells that go *jingle-jangle-jingle*.
The butterflies are free to
fly, and so sweet child are we.

The alluring flames do burn deep.
To beckon a call for intimacy
I sing to what resonates in me.
In my finest hour I feel the native
pulse flowing through;
so happily, so lively, it shows;
so happily, so lovely, we grow.

I am a cloud catcher
endearing as the redwood;
agile as the leopard;
clean as the crystal falls;
well trekked as a whale;

keen sighted as an eagle;
and everywhere the wind blows.

The grand illusion of progress
is a formidable pursuit.
The village voice cries out for
the no name hero.
Passions of the time needle him.
    Must we call upon him?
    Must we smile upon him?
At his break point must we pity him?

To what end do we bargain with he
who stirs the bitches brew in the
disparaging name of country news?
False ideas emanate from a rat hole
most foul and corrupt. I see a simple
orchid bloom nestled in a
dark forest.

The blood of innocence is poured
into a white marble box gliding
up the aisle of Christ. The death
spell of a child thins the air. I have
found my black tulip, my purple
rose, in a place where gray skies
blanket me in mortuary.

A boy sits in the doorway of a
heart attack in progress. He spies
a pale gray man locked into a
catatonic state. His wife sponged his
brow until the ambulance arrived.
I tossed the portrait of his death
in the attic.

In my experience, the blood in
the fields simply vaporized into
confederates in the attic. The
eyelids of Dixie expose the black
note lunatic bouts of hatred cold

and naked. This portrait of despair
was taken by blue angels who
were never human.

In truth, lies the fantasy of romance;
in word, my bloodline will last long
after the Roman Aqueducts crumble
to dust. We are lost in a dream of
frontier: the undiscovered country;
the promised land; king's without
fear; walls without ears. And
we shall witness a foul stage.

Hamlet the Dane played in a
bone yard lost in name. The
anguish of the man torn apart
by his countries false heart.
The skull-ed millennium visions
of his undiscovered country.
The death of the bog queen.
The jester lost his will to laugh.

The refugee's blood trail ends in a
muddy field leached in generational
lies. The children of poverty are
waiting on a solution that may never
come; a hard testament to live by.
The sands of time will bury lost lives.
The loveless cry deaf tears.

The wild orchid's crown sweats in
desires of affection. Run, run seasons
run; run wild on earthly incense.
A marshmallow fog spirals off a lake
blackened still. The pixie queen dances
blind with the devil out in the
moonlight grin. Run, run fables, run . . .

The lantern balloons float out into a
loveless atmosphere. Golden
illuminations fan out in this season

of hell and sail off to a distant shore.
You give us love, love, love, in the
gray moon shrine. O rise, rangers rise,
rise above these pools of suspicion.
Sail on, Lady Lovelace, with grand
illusions.

The society rags taut delectable
edibles and material ornaments
of achievement, known as; *bling,
bling*, or rather, *bring, bring!*
The impersonal yet focal tour
of the flesh blights us. Celebrity
winks and smiles as trouble
ripples in the moonshine.

The fashion news daily spins a web
of privilege and deceit;
that metro chic velvet fog that
smothers reality in all of its quality.
The botox pickle of a model with
her eyes painted black.
Remember that stoic frail pose of
a gypsy, in mud rain, that made
you feel dead inside?

You were reduced to a novelty
and placed on the shelf in the local
library. Your dreams threatened by
those who would burn books to
promote their own self importance.
A smoke that thunders stardust
memories. You are the blood ore
of America. You will not be forgotten.

The death of some small victory for
humanity will touch the brazen palm
of the urban hustle with sad humility;
albeit, the shining flowers of grief.
   We have bronzed ourselves.
   We have bled ourselves.

We have lost ourselves.

The insolent cobra eyes strike;
bloodshot on white, and
the walls came tumbling down.
The Oedipus of evil.
I think I know why the crowd shouts.
I think I know why their shouldn't
be any doubt.
      I think I know!

The terrorist can sustain itself on
a dollar a day. He can act with lethal
consequences for a few dollars more.
The clerics speak with vile intentions;
on fist of fury, on hope of prayer;
it rips at the social fabric of
community. And they call it,
 "the pious stench of repair".

A life of broken promises lies
scattered along the walkway. The
calamity of life driven at the stake.
A kink in the armor does not score
a mortal wound. The dust settles
in the endless night. And only Seamus
knows the serenity of the farming
community with its drowned cat.
And in the end we all push up daisies.

The wolves of plunder feed off of the
satanic face of misery. Humanity,
in all of its torn fury bleeds.
The sands of time shroud in mystery
a porous sod that weeps.
Through the looking glass I see
the sins of the past repeat and still
      I wonder why!

The heretics' beliefs lie beneath

the gods and monsters.
The cultural caldron stirs in a
garden of good and evil.
An appetite for intolerance
bleeds the sage.
Tears, big hot tears, blur my vision
of a garden of Eden.

I fly down a timber road breaking
hard into a controlled slide-stop
in beaver town. The pond boy's cue
with satisfied impressions. A camp fire
creeps out of its pit. I try to smother
the smoldering embers. Smoke frenzied
yellow jackets dive bomb me; one stings
me on the thigh, I guess I had it coming.

The bronzed ballerina awaits her
introduction with a tarnished
heart held a world apart; devoted
in principle, to a fairytale of love,
laughter and elegance. She is like a
Chess Master, with a maternal order
in mosaic tapestry passing through
the tremor of time; sublime passion
with eloquent passages.

And if you close your eyes does it almost
feel like something died inside?
And if it looks like the heavens move slowly,
 I'd like to count that night in her dreams.
And if you've been keeping secret fires,
 I'd like to touch the flames' release.
And so she contemplates the art of living,
like the Willow in the wind, with
stormy eyes that turn sympathetic
if your heart is true.

You made me fall in love and I bleed
all over it; looking out or within
I see nonsensical suicides.

I know I'm only dreaming; but,
in her eyes I see a little dream of need
and I will be holding it close to mine.
I will embrace her until the end of time.
I will until our ashes all fall down.
        I will!   I will!

Amazing what an image can do.
Amazing what a village can do.
Amazing what a free spirit
can peek through. The kids
will need us to fight the mortal
thief with furious daring do.
A portal of confessions is less
than they deserve; so, strangers,
if you bleed . . .

Celluloid heroes work the land-
scape by day and by night.
The ruby-red sunset glimmers
before giving way to darkness;
a light of beauty and bitterness.
Tender is the night in the
moonlit gallery of black and white.
In one fell swoop we let those
sleeping lies die.

My thoughts reach out for
some kind of wonderful;
would that be you?
You can see the burning flames.
You can feel my pain.
You can reach out and touch me.
You can know my name:
you can, *y o u c a n!*

The folk singer plays to a run
away melody and that song runs
along until it meets its natural end.
And we listen to the folk art
of his stories. And we feel better

for it, for he passes this way like a
slow parade of little black rain clouds
or moonlit masquerades.

In the golden days of motion picture
novelty, the camera had its own
personality. The poets, players, and
muses, all performed good folklore;
tears of a flower, howls beat through
the hours; no fear, no butcher,
all were empowered. To kill a name
one must walk through the shadows
and write the songs that people dream.

In the long blue acid melody
we see the relevance of
this late night rhapsody.
A dragon's molten breathe in
the red moon desert.
The pale cape of the anointed
saints will plot their escape.
The body politic has failed
to see the consequences.

We see the musicians and poets
all along the freedom trail trying
hard not to look too frail.
Cry a little song for me.
I am real…does love not cry?
Helpless trespasses.
Seductive compassion.

The eyes of the jaded roil sin for
one more go in the valley below.
The eyes of Mt. Rushmore sneer.
I pass into the eve of time.
I roam beyond the dome of night.
I see all the dark.
I see all the light.
I wonder as I wander.

I wonder why the faded glory
of our epic stories dissolved
into the songs of silence.
The sentimental journey gently weeps.
The bedrock of our civilization
may crack but it holds firm.
The Visigoths sacked Rome.
The Conquistadors sacked the Aztecs.
The Allies sacked Berlin.

I wonder if we will be done in.

I penetrate the great escape.
The cog head caught in a ghost
machine; far beneath the sea,
where the neon ornaments glow;
a realism far beyond the fantasy
of a wild picture show. In the silent
indigo fusion, I witness a placid
neon symphony.

I wander into a dream scape
filled with silent screams.
The pale elegance of mannequins
are mirrored over the faceless
lake of community in a
cage of lifeless beauty. And still
my heart gently weeps for the
solitary leopard in the night air.

Ansels' gallery of shape shifters
share cloud kisses in Yosemite
National Park. The pale gray
laughter haunts me in my silent
way. Restless sprites howl along
the edge of night. A fold reared
in the forest's lining. I'm wide
awake and night is *fa*
                              ll
                       ing.

The Moth Man's execution is
commuted. The sinner is trapped
in his madness. And he will bear
the hangman's noose, as a necktie,
for the rest of his life. He will
carry that weight for a long time;
no parole, no saving grace for
his gallery of horror. The death
of ash babies cry mud tears.

I offer a song of myself.
Can you not hear in the shadows
and fog? This, the song of myself,
I sing to those who would hear;
to those whom I hold most dear;
a multidimensional song of myself
most vivid and true. Why are
the gods and monsters so cruel?

A placid biography pours in
red light, blue light
lunatic rants of catastrophe.
The lunatic warrior ghost offers
the disgrace of an evangelist.
The hungry child's proclamation.
Angels and demons,
in her heart, love dances blue.
The night fever junk ally sojourns find
body tremors sweating bourbon.

Applied structures ripping skin;
tattoo parlor legions of
lotus blossoms in mud rain.
In the cold fusion, volcanic erections
falling off the nova ledge.
Tangled, twisted, and stateless
our bronzed souls leak
lunar tide pools of suspicion.
Our lunatic pride hell bent on

invention.

A constellation of dreams is falling
into grief. The unsavory savage
will kick off sweet and tender
mercies. He hides behind reticent
eyes of unspeakable truths and
common lies. Tangerine dreams
must form the conduit for
our planet news.

Bull whims skull around in the
promised garden and death
surrounds the clock towers.
Tears of a flower are set
adrift in the wake. And that
federal metronome depresses
me in my silent way.

I sing for the lonesome dove
hiding in the shadows.
I sing for the hummingbirds
in the magnolia trees.
I sing for the lost children of
    K a t r i n a.
I sing it by day,
  I sing it by night,
    I sing it with passionate delight.

Forgive us this day our whimsical
tapestries. On this day we master
the illusion of integrity.
Little by little, we share in the
laurels of nobility. The sweet
land of liberty singing freely;
   of thee I sing.

The deep moral conscience of
a blessed promise;
one place, one whole world,

the old one and the new,
recycled and renewed:
a cycle of life bold yet askew.
Why does the rustic wanderer breathe
in a big room of stars?

The mystical solar orchestra awakes.
Fluent solar winds brush the
millennium ash of humanity.
Baby stars shoot out of a black
hole delivering diamond light from
a distant corner. The optical rhythms
play for a bright new age.

We are the world if you please
or if you don't please.
What am I to all of this?
Truth be told, I'm no better than you,
so sing with me a heartfelt song;
let it not fall on deaf ears;
have no fear,
      let it sound out,
           let it endear.

July 2003 – Feb 2014

Sing Low

The faceless lake of
  community

The race of melodies
  fluid flow

The song bird faces
  bitterness

Sing low, sing low song bird
  let it go

The burning kiss of
  a sweet love divine

You can't touch tenderness
  willfully

Sing low, sing low song bird
  let it go

April 2004

Sweet Favor

Sweet favor shines
    full and bright

Resting easy in
    the rising storm

In pursuit of
    guiding light

A lover's eve
    on golden pond

Sweet favor shines
    full and bright

All my worries
    drift on air

Tracking solo
    in white sands

Reflections in
    starry light

Freedom's kiss does
    feel right

Sweet favor shines
    full and bright

March 2004

Gothic Moonrise

The kids of the blacken gray
strut in rut at the city malls,
scavenging in crow style,
scoffing at the world colored in style.
The berated stoic face painted gray,
charcoal eyes, tearing a black rain.
A death face abated.
The body cushion pinned in silver.
The body art is in abscess.
The body dielectric stained black.
Rage against the machine.
Rage against family needs.
Rage against humor.
Rage against the good seed.
The Gothic moonrise bleeds.
The myth o satanic verse choking
off the neon-charges of life.
The howl of the night beacons you;
no, not me, you go in my stead!
I believe in a world of color:
in peaked pinks, in rosy blushes,
in steel blues, in silvery flashes,
in golden hues, in natural tones;
all in fluid strokes to beguile.
One world, our world, colored in style.
A Gothic pox is upon us
as the fatalist red dawn arises.

October 2003

Ghost Town
(For Bill Frisell)

A desolate old shanty town
has lost its way.
The fluid skin of summer,
blackened gray, as the folks
strayed. Now a place with
a permanent frown. Even
the post has stopped
their rounds.

Main street is littered and
everything seems pillaged.
A pack of dogs on the prowl.
The blustery wind only howls
a mad song in whispers:
quietly, we prey for no more lies.

Ages ago this community thrived;
somehow, its lifeblood tapped out.
Life was finally spent.
The tears of restless spirits rain
of love lost, hear its echo;
please save me, relate to me.

Many families rooted here
when earlier cues were sincere;
tradition, will be accounted for
in this sordid chorus.
The aging cemetery tells a tale
of splendor, washed away in tears.

Veteran graves
marked with tattered flags;
eternal resting spots
organized by family plots.
These bones shall rise again!
The folks that built

ole town square were;
carpenters, ministers, leaders,
criers, and cheaters, teachers,
poets, lovers, farmers,
heroes, and singers.

Folks of all shades where
abandoned by their own kin.
A reckoning must be held here
at Ghost Town.
Troubled spirits for sale?
Our love spent in life's blood!
The town now lies
drowning in its own mud.

O beckon to hear the
echoes of a crowded cheer.
Celebrations of life with
the star dust shown bright.
A mood filled with love,
laughter and elegance.

A rain swept flowers curtsy.
A place long foreshadowed,
all but forgotten. O please, please,
relieve this shanty towns' tired heart;
a lost place with a sacred start.

The whispers tell me you're leaving.
What more can I do?

April 2003

Medusa

(For Bjork)

Mystical illuminations defy
  the laws of physics.
A pit-fired slide show
  of personnel passages.
The ornaments of achievement
  sparkle proudly.
The incantations ring
  out loud.

Medusa's eternal curse
  was a serpent's lair
    painted black.
The titan stone-eyed lash.
I know why the caged girl
    screams.
The genteel lady love lace
    bleeds.
And I know why lost love
    dreams.

Through the looking glass,
  I've seen, the wonders of life
    come to pass.
The celestial abstracts
  of triumph and defeat.
I know where the
  silver angels roam.
I noticed that they are
  not alone.

The anointed savior of the
  eternal light orchestra.
A crystal landscape reflects
  our right of passage.
The red velvet ladies perform
  wild wind flower dances.

The pendant charm of a
   dragon star sheds fire light
   on the artistic eye.

   February 2005

Everlasting
(For Columbine High)

Put me away dressed in white cotton linens,
positioned head-n-hand, pointed at the molten core;
cleaned, dried and wrapped.

As a dried sack of beans I could sprout
and take root. My satchel-ed body
will merely linger underfoot.

What will they make of me?
Will they make a mockery of me?
Will they make a monument of me?

Am I now reduced to a motto,
a slogan, a parceled verse?
Will I be remembered or cursed?

I've shed my last drop of blood, sweat, tear;
I have no regrets , I'm all ears.
My only wish is that they wrapped me well.

I have no wish to become beetle dung.
I wish to remain relevant, in the lives,
that have so touched me; that will do,

that will do, if not for an eternity too.
Which one of us is supple with joy beyond
the boundaries of a new born namesake?

I'll release my epithet into a fresh landscape.
I wish that I created the syllabic tags of a new
symbolic language that paints a vivid picture;
in mood, in ambiance, in lore.

My veins are merely mortal.
My writings are a kind of time portal,
regressing deep, from humble beginnings.

I've enjoyed the energy of the sun;
I've stood eye lids shut, facing it, seeing
the red hue of my blood flowing through.

See the kaleidoscope of colors
reflected against my eye lids;
a somber mood never looked so vivid.

I do not believe in conditional love.
I am fortified with salient introspection,
to be any less, would be so slovenly pup.

I do not wish for my children to be prodigies,
merely exceptional, at their chosen pursuits;
lovingly satisfied, in life, and with me.

I trust that they will be able to reason their way
around the demon who wields a spitfire gun.
A blind rage ready to snuff out a wonderful life
in a single strike; if only to escape their perpetual strife;

that will do, that most definitely, will do!
If I have failed to achieve this bonding relationship,
you may spit at me; you may regard me as shrewd;

that will do, that will have to do,
for I am finally through; as for my love,
it will travel with you.

May 2003

The Makeshift Paragon
(For Conor Oberst)

A corporeal life feeds
  the undiscovered countries'
    demolition;
quick silver,
  the smoke that billows a sigh...
Beneath the cities foundation,
  wrapped in a layered bed of time,
    a profoundness once stood.
The dew drops on the flora
  are the sum of its tears.
The human stain caught
  in the ramparts of this world.
I wander the places of good parlor
  and at once, time ripples.
The shadows pantomime good faith
And what for the planets to align?
In my escape,
  I once heard a somber song and
    my fingers turned cold.
The makeshift delinquency.
A cardinal in the cherry tree sings.
O, do not take notice of him;
  he kisses the wind with such
    bittersweet sorrow.
The contagious black terror,
  kisses the blade,
    in manic rants of catastrophe.
 The makeshift lynx-eye in
  a frontier that always smiles:
    here where all of me runs;
      here where all of me stops:
        the philosophy of greed
          d e c a y s.
The penitent one shuffles around
  like the cardinal in a moldy town.
The makeshift paragon lost in a world

turning upside down;
Aches, aches, we all fall down,
Aches, aches, we all fall down. . . .

March 2005

P.S. My beagle ate your autographed picture.

Suspended

A life suspended, scared by
  the secret ways of our lives.
The melancholy hours are marked
  by the wilted flowers.
Every day, I look at the broken
  pieces. I hear the spoken teases.
I don't care what comes next
  and I don't even care
    if it's against all good bets.
If you want to take a stand
  you just call out my name.

My baby lies over the rainbow.
My body lies over the moon.
If I could reach out I surely would.
   Wouldn't I? Could I?
I can hear the electric blues
  of the night.
I get the news as I wander by.
I wonder what is so funny
  about a peaceful harmony.

The anxious reflections
  of my glass menagerie
    seek out the prairie of truth.
My neighbor paints love
  as plaid as a dimpled pimp.
I paint love in a
  passionate constellation.

I am living with ghosts,
  lifeless, gray ghosts.

What if I can only see
  the perfection of love?
Will I be able to hear
  its chorus?

Will I be able to feel
  its devotion?
Will I ever know
  its divinity?

I wonder as I wander in
A waterfall of cares pouring
  over the millstone.
Do I frighten you? No.
  I hope I don't!

November 2004

Time Square

the gravity of Time Square
the amusement of Broadway
with its light box sway
a romantic tinsel kiss
on a monster billboard blitz
the tempo of quick silver
promises to deliver
the finery, the oddities,
the loveless fall like dominoes
and that's just how it goes
does anyone ever really make
eye contact with one another

September 2006

Inhibitions

My fear is my only blind fold
  or so I'm told; but for today,
    it would seem like table scraps.

Last night I was on my guard as
  the flames flashed forward, smoke-in-ash;
    I dream a little scream of me.

Tested in soiled surroundings,
  I wonder how it is to be prouder?
I ease a little spin on me.

I skip stones in a still water pond
  basking in the sounds of silence;
    I seek a little meek on me.

What is this feeling of mine?
Initially, I thought that I was failing;
  I shed a little burden unto me.

I handle a scorpion in the desert,
  feeling pure and clean in desolation;
    I don a little shield on me.

Look long and you will see
  that I am reticent.
I grant a little wish formally.

I pass through the crystal falls and
  stand naked to a cause;
    I stir up a little pulse in me.

Just because, just because.

October 2003

Tatters

The fragility of a butterfly knows not
what lies ahead; freely it flutters,
in sun soaked floral beds.

I find the monotony of the social
debauchery alarming as the quills
of a porcupine influenced by curiosity.

The mind in tatters conjures no notion
of familiar matters.
        "I detest; no, I protest it!"

The rigor of duplicity quickly fades.
The jagged edge of the spiny shore
hewed by the rolling surf; my blood cools-

My life longs for sacred keepsakes.
I'll rejoice in the abusers faded flop.
I'll blast through the hallmark haunts

in the brazen tick of the social click.
A boy's will bent into crooked ills?
Holding on to it I brood.
        I'm shattered!

November 2003

Sylvia

"Sylvia, who turned out the lights?"
A loaded eye with a keen
natural bream. An elegant
deliberate habit shear
deadening in suspense.

Your erratic nerve was delicately
 prone to serve, in verse;
verse by verse, in a tangled curse.
The telling signs of a dangerous mind.
"O Sylvia, let the sun shine in."

Let me help you clear your mind
you may be missing an important find;
lyrically congested, you feel rejected.
You must avoid the traps of a deafening despair,
life is formidable, but hardly fair.

With your suffering complete
and your horizons shown bleak;
dwell not in unnatural affairs for
pain is never a solitary affair.
You must tolerate human frailty!

Your mommy wouldn't do and
your daddy was already through.
Dear daddy was stern and lovingly
satisfied with you; why would he try
to get back at you?

"Calling Sylvia, O Sylvia!"

A dreadful silence, I fear its too late.
Your verse is hard to contemplate.
Your essence inspires me to relate;
deep in feeling, unsettled in nerve;
forever, the tigress who tempted fate.

Spiraling inward:
bothered, bewildered, caged in tight;
dazed, you're unable to put up a fight;
tragically, you missed your guiding light;
"Goodnight Sylvia, Goodnight."

O how the night must move!

March 2003

Predestine Journey
(For Keb' Mo')

 I struggle with an emptiness
   deep and low down.
We'll make tracks for open spaces;
    'cause, smiling faces fill empty spaces.

On a journey of destiny
   the sweat will get in my eyes
     and I won't wonder why.
I want more than to just get by.

There are places and things
   that I should know by heart.
Places in the heart where
   I could get off to a good start.

The bitter sting of fear
   places you in arrears.
A hapless life caught in a trap
   with no way back.

I know I'm only dreaming
 but I can't let go.
I know I'm moving
 much too slow.

I am lost and I admit it:
 my destination is unknown.
I look back on my will
  cast in stone.

What I'm saying is that
   I'll make it on my own.

              January 2004

Withering Hearts

Moonlight peeks through
the snow flurries; in the
twilight's glow, a bareness
shows through to the necessity
of love's labored laughter.

The blustery winds blanket me
in my silent way. My passions
cool to a stoic face, pale gray.
Life as a frozen canvas, a
screaming will lies here still.

The chickadees busily perform
a crazy foot dance, foraging
for feed. The momentum of
muscle memory paces them
through their day. O what a
fool they must take me for.

I wonder why you don't hear
my stories?
Maybe, I'll never know or
perhaps you just stopped trying;
I don't know;
      I need you,
      I bleed you!
I grow tired of this isolation!

Why aren't you tempted
to hear my stories?
I see your silhouette against the
fullness of the snow moon
            and I'm tempted.

February 2004

Blown Glass

The flash furnace smooths
the jagged edges blown
true to form.

The heated flow of
liquid glass is shaped into
    a goblet,
      a lantern, or
        an hour glass.

The mellow gold phosphor of
a crystalline structure glows;
the tributaries of memory
freely flow.

The crystal lattice is cracked:
distortions in prism reveal

the paramour of hypocrisy.
Molten jabs fade to black;
my heart melts to liquid jack.

March 2004

Birdsong

A bird sings.
The ladybird lies
on broken wing;
  unwilling,
    unable,
      to answer
the call to mate.
The male bird sings
  a melody,
    a promise;
      to nest,
        to behold.
The stolen season
has grown cold.
O listen to hear
the merry melody;
  singing,
    whistling;
      my pretty,
        my dear,
          play tell,
            do appear.

June 2003

Stones

a labyrinth of glacial stone deposits
laid to rest

the geologic sculptures adorn
the old growth forest

a monolith juts out of its natural gallery
a lone head caps the column

the sweeping shadows change face
the granite king turns sedate

a crystalline lens of water falls past
the out workings of a lost cathedral

a colossal granite bedrock forges
the allure of lost utopian civilizations

December 2003

Luck Be A Stone Lion

A new dawn arises
on the perilous pride
of forsaken namesake

in the shade of an acacia
tree, young lions feed on
a baby giraffe

the flame-orange haze of
an African sun melts
the horizons steady line

the distant roar of the
alpha cats are always
answered by rifled shots

the stone predator is
part of the great rhythm
of our natural life

the holes in habitat
must be patched or we will
have seen our last wild scratch

the village tribe must avoid
the temptation eyes of
the jungle pride

lifeless stone eyed trophies
and sleeper clones may just
well be what remains of

the stone lions perilous way
luck be a lion tonight
luck be a stone lion tonight

August 2004

Frenchman's Reef

A harbor buoy clangs as the gulls jut out
the sun burns off remnants of a pale fog

steely waves crash the breakers
a salt spray fills the air

fast and lively the sounds of revelry
a fisherman's tale

baiting hooks strung out like Christmas lights
marker buoys set with strobe lights

packing fish stakes on ice
a barrel fire is stoked by nightfall

a cold chop tosses the boat about
a fisherman never ails

the captain sets course for the home port
Frenchman's Reef, all hail

September 2003

Star Turtle

(for Harry Connick, Jr.)

Lost cities run blood red.
O' star turtle,
   come back to my world;
intrepid mariner of the starry night.
I'm outbound,
   'till my eyes see right.

Shine on 'till tomorrow,
   I will be here again;
wipe away your sorrow,
   a majestic motif relates.

I walk the waterfront.
   I'm dancing all alone.
I'm flying ever higher.
   My heart is already gone.

I gaze at the stars seeing the epicycles
of diamond light.
I spin around to create a kaleidoscope.
The star turtle kisses me.

Am I stronger then I believe?
And baby, you didn't know me then.

                July 2004

Pemigewasset River
(Franconia Notch State Park, NH)

The Pemigewasset
river runs swift and cold;
pure and supple.

A good day sunshine.
The stout treed forest echoes
sensual rhythms.

Vanilla winds
flavor our field of views
palm discovery.

Magnetic dreams pen
the etchings of millennia, where
aged impressions live.

A good day blind. We
listen to the winds wash away
the urban hustle.

The crystal basin
forges the mirrored challis of
bountiful passages.

A good day find at
the river running swiftly, cold,
pure and supple.

January 2005

Black Cat
(for Jim Hendrix)

The black cat voodoo wild
embraces the psychedelic night;
black cat, excuse me if I shun
the sky.

Did you ever loose faith before
you ran out of time?
You played those acid blue notes
that raged against the body politic.

In your eyes we saw the ghost in the
machines; purple haze was on the rise,
with mellow moonbeams twisting lies.

The crystal windows among the stars
reflect messages to play on our minds
with no vibe that hasn't been tried.

The shadow puppets trained their eyes
on the star dust wondering if the
black cat would sketch his intentions...

A lake of sadness rippled through the night
blackened still; excuse me, if I kiss the sky.

November 2004

The Ugly Waltz

The ugly waltz.

A bird on a hot tin roof,
   dances,
the ugly waltz.

 A full moon cycles
  the night sky, behind
the bird on a hot tin roof;
   dancing,
the ugly waltz.

The crickets sing in jubilee,
   as a full moon cycles the night sky;
behind, the bird on a hot tin roof;
   dancing,
the ugly waltz.

The rain drops drum a beat
  as the crickets sing in jubilee.
A full moon cycles the night sky;
behind, the bird on a hot tin roof;
   while it dances,
the ugly waltz.

The night falls silent.
The rain stops falling on the
   crickets who sang with glee.
The full moon completes its cycle
   behind a vacant tin clad roof.
The clown has flown away.

Only the lonely see it that way.

March 2005

Grammy
(No, I never had a Grammy)

The lady of the sun dried cottage wares
  a pink dress laced in leopard trim
    with a floral-clad straw hat.
A film of bee's wax seals her lips;
this lily is lathered well, for a
  sunny soak, in a bed of stones. Her
    cobalt eyes set aglow in the red dawn;
a will of imagery is born.
"O, Grammy, what do you see?"
I see sketches of Spain lost in your
  enduring pain. No, I've never been
    to Spain, but I'd kind of like to get there.
"Is it at all like Miles Davis' musical notes?"
"Is it like the Spaniard floats in the town parade?"
"Was your heart broken or mended?"
A road lost to a Spaniard mystery.

O beloved goddess!
You make my world a better place.
The LOVE is not lost on you,
    you bore it well:
        fair the well;
        faith can tell.

          October 2003

Anne
(For Anne Frank)

What is love if not kin to favor?
One love, you give me fever;
a fever flash in rash behavior.

My love is full of pain, as a
teacher, you're insane! Foolish
fever crying in black rain.

At times, I feel like we should kiss;
then again, I think we wouldn't click;
but then I feel like we couldn't miss.

Maybe, I just don't understand.
Maybe, I must learn to trust my instincts.
Maybe, love is just filled with conflict.

I often wish we were in love,
not in a friendship sort of way;
but all the way,

like when your heart is eclipsed
with a song on your lips,
and a poem at your finger tips.

Love, O rueful, careless love,
will not stand in judgment
somewhere beyond the sea.

One love is an ageless letter for
when you're in love, you're in forever;
embrace it faithfully.

You're in love with the way
if you truly believe in
what you say;

more than you,
> more than me,
>> more than fervid memory.

The simple facts of love do ring true;
embrace me, I'm right where
I'm suppose to be.

May 2003

Venus If You Will

(for Barbra Streisand)
A crescent moon rides
motherly breast of Venus
nurturing the eye.

The shiny nipple,
a nurturing focal point
in the starry night.

The pride of passion
pours over me adorning
a gracious new face.

The lover's new name.
A leopard lies with the dove
in a naked spot.

A singular hope,
Aphrodite's golden rope
eternally bound.

The beast of burden
bearing the rim of the night
sky on his shoulders.

The corona of
a heart's desire flash cooled
in cleansing sea foam.

A new hope rises
out of the sea bath, singing
a great love song.

The motherly breast
of Venus riding the crest
nurturing the eye.

March 2004

Pearl Diver

(For Hollie Smith)

Pearl divers weeping.
The mother of black pearls leak
the jewel of time.

Wind chimes sing for the
beautiful looser in the
midnight gallery.

The steel tulips
rusted by the dark shadows
of lonesome pathways.

Nightingales sing
a song in rapture over
crystal lip river.

A river of dreams
pours over me; a thunder
from a distant shore.

Crystalline shores kiss
the body challis of charged
timeless passages.

Oceans of fire.
The house of the rising sun
plays passionately.

Moon light seems right for
the children of the bonfires
feeling messages.

August 2004

Secret Garden

Why do I own
  the misery of us?
    You stomp

on the goodness
  of the polished pearl
    in a requiem for a girl;

the high crimes
  and misdemeanors
    of the cursed heart.

I place your
  stormy eye
    in its tinder box;

if you walk out of
  my life maybe
    it will hit me.

O,
  why do I believe
    in this paradox?

I ask you
  what kind of love
    ever does?

The miserable tide lost
  in the way of a
    wrangled pride.

The pearl moon is down,
  made to disappear,
    in a handful of dust.

You can blame it on

broken dreams but
   why put up the fuss?

I thought you were a
  silhouette on the wall;
    cold and featureless.

We were so tired
  of being small, so
    bring it on one and all.

 In the secret garden
  of wholesome delight;
    sky larks are in flight:

butterflies dance with
  the whippoorwills, as
    lady marble blows kisses.

The miracle of love's
  laughter. Will you
    sing with me some how?

The secret garden floats
  in a moon river
    of black velvet.

The midnight gallery
  is its own avenger.
I dare not speak of it.

January 2005

Dueling Dragons

Silhouette forgets
the base rhythms of lime light;
the passions red flair.

Naked whispers spit.
Bipolar impressions flood
the virgin landscape.

The heart palpitates.
A river runs into its wake.
The black notes escape.

The blood orchid knows.
Twisting dragons in thin air.
A wanton despair.

Far, far and away
our demons tare us apart;
the dust of broken hearts.

In blood memory
the art of dueling dragons
imitate chaos.

The liar's pin cushion.
A manic rush of the head;
labored concussions.

Homespun memories.
The heart that knows the answers.
Star bright confetti.

August 2004

A Plaid Style

I am mad as a hornet
if only for a moment
red ribbons on paper dolls
blue velvet whisper calls

tangerine harp dreams
stark howling screams
gray ghosts stew
in rain cloud brews

unrequited ruby love
soils the ivory dove
sun portraits beckon
our faint heart-ed lesson

the mandarin sun halos
over powder cloud bellows
strike a pose of casualty
in our primrose reality

I see a silhouette
on the wall of regret
it is your plaid style
that makes me smile

June 2006

A Ruby Desire
(for the girly ghost in the park)

The ruby desire of spider love,
in her heart, love dances blue.
Rembrandt's gallery of ivory tiles
form in mosaic to a civil travesty.

The confessions of rue liaisons
drip in pearl petals. The supple taste
of ruddy rain drops off a tea leaf lingers.

My blood memory drips into mellow
sweet tide pools; tin lip kisses find me
in the shadow of monotony,
cold and seamless.

The death of the idealist.
The myth of the guardian angel:
a seedless nature has crossed my
mind many times.

A pearl moon dots the skyline
in the purple haze of dusk.
The day is packed with
far away tears.

Healthy squirrels accept salt peanuts
from a child in the park. The child is
a self proclaimed ghost; but she allows
you to see her, and to play ball with her.

The poet locked in the attic
with his heart of molten glass.
The sage laments! A day lost to the wild
orchid; you're beautiful, it's true.

An opal river laces through the parks greenery.
 The ugly duckling is nowhere in sight.

The swan boat tourists admire the scenery.
The aroused pigeons take flight.

A time for little black rain clouds in
a birth in funeral. A portal
of flash memories wrap around
mythical corners.

The pathos of a surrealist are sketches
of inherited truth. No sleeping
in the park today by order
of the commonwealth.

No dancing in the park
until I feel as good as you;) I sing
a melancholy blue to satisfy a
savage itch.

A girls' bare midriff is lined with
milk fat; she dances in
the park to the weather maker's
hustle and flow.

I play to the lost chronicles
of the stone. The castle in the clouds
is defended by an army of you.
The journey of the songbird

is calling; will you protect the child's
dream in the park?
Here I dance barefoot in the park
with supernatural children...
      1, 2, 3 go!

Do we frighten you 'cause we
hope we don't!

May 2006

New Moon Cabin

the new moon cabin rests easily on
the bossa nova shore
after tea and tango we listen to jazz
under the mango tree
we listen to the quite pulse
of a blissful evening
the moth girl glimmers in the moonshine
she sings her heart in earnest
the silk worms delicately spin a web
of my meditative state
a view through silken lens reveals
a white lotus smile in mud rain
fireflies flash in sweet melody
black smiles on sweet revelry
we play charades by fire light
baring clues in the moon shadows
nothing but starry skies do I see
on this myopic sage fantasy

May 2006

Don't You Weep

As I recall, I found out that I am
thrilling no one but I do insist
that there be some meaning.

We play on the sweetness of the day
and trek into a reckless night; impatiently,
waiting on a breathless melody.

A desolate red fox scurries along the
water's edge and pauses to witness our
coded rhythms.

Why do we mark our time like the
quick fox? We make small tangerine
dreams look like *film noir* screams.

A fog laces over our scandalous fallacy;
afterwords, we gaze at the starry night
feeling so contrite.

I feel sympathetic to those who
see with tunnel vision. After all,
what did the thunder say?

Am I being shaken out of my dream?
I am on a path divided from the rest
of me from here to eternity.

I alone hand out white roses
to a crowd moved by the promise
of a hot wet kiss;

I get to the next one
and on to the next one
and so on down the line.

The fragrance of reality blends into
the sirens of emergency;

looking out or looking in,

I spy nonsensical suicides;
I stop it dead, beating the Devil's rot
in this season of Hell.

O dark angel, why do you billow
smoke, outrageously, over our
golden metropolis?

That is more than I can take!
That is more than you can take!
I awake to a gilded chorus singing

gospel from their ivory towers;
if only, to connect the dots of
senselessness.

The world will be your oyster and
you shall reap what you sow.
I hate that fortune cookie rap!

O amazing grace and grim, is it
simple to see the crossroads?
Why do the stars continue to shine?

You loose your kaleidoscope dreams
over your glacial habits. The loveless fall like
dominoes and that's just how it goes.

I set adrift in the faceless lake of
community where I find a graveyard
filled with fail-safe lunacy.

O but don't you weep for me.
I must find myself along the way as
I learn to live in a healthy sadness.

April 2006

Cloud Catcher

(Mt. Washington hike)

The misty mourning
sun gently rises above
the cloud pools.

The granite bedrock
pokes through the smokey brew;
mixing grays, greens, and blues.

The waterworks run
the colossal bowl's inner rim;
cleansing scents on air.

A blanket of ice
sweats into the heat of summer,
shrink warping on stones.

The cloudy halo's
cool mist soothes a troubled
wind walkers dry bones.

A head in the clouds
masked from horizons on far,
stands a mile high.

July 2004

Paper Moon

(For Diana Krall & Elvis Costello)

Narrow moon light
  enters my room.
The paper moon folds
  midnight into noon.

Dangerous namesakes float past
  the shallow moon;
  once, weary to the bone over
  scattered stepping stones.

The marble eyes of
  the nocturnal babies
  see caged impressions
  along the edge.

The nightingale's game is
  a sweet love song; forevermore.
The faceless lake of community
  struggles to relate.

The pale moon reflects
  the night owl's desperado.
The rain shadows flow in
  the mania of vertigo.

The desert rose sheds
  its embroidery on
  the tremor of time.
The black stone gallery

  is sublime. The withering
  lights. The owl's eyes pulse
    like fireflies.
The never lasting dawn was

  a paper moon; after all,

I would not stand for it,
not even on the loose
by the next nightfall.

October 2004

Portraits
(casual observations)

               I
two contortionist entangled
in a plexiglass cube

              II
a crows bloody beak spits

             III
a mother and baby bobbing
in a pool whispering sweet nothings

             IV
a squirrel gouging a pumpkin
for its seed

             V
a single flower flows through
black water canals in
Brick Town

             VI
girls pretending to be on calls
in the air terminal are actually
spying my every move

             VII
banana winds
  strawberry fields
    mandarin sunsets
lemon squeezes
  cherry kisses

             VIII
kids dashing through cotton
sheets hung out to dry

IX
tiger lilies choke feebler hedgerows
black oaks cry tears of a flower

X
hatch-lings whistle a hungry tune

XI
the white noise of a crystal falls
sounded for millennium and only the
next ice age may silence it

XII
a bronzed ballerina awaits her
introduction

XIII
where have all the flower girls gone?

XIV
a dolphin in a nursery fends off hands
pawing at their sensitive spot

XV
the silhouette of rain dancers kiss
a pearl drop moon

XVI
squirrels cart off corn husks
in a mid-summers' dry dusk

XVII
kids swat at fireflies with tennis rackets
on the fatal trajectory a bright lemon
glow turns to lime then it fades to black
after impact

XVIII
a woodpecker zipper taps at dawn
~pauses~

then resumes its coded rhythms

XIX
fluent ivory rose dancers embrace
the gray moon shrine
a thespian winks and smiles

XX
the hoot owl hollers partly sublime

XXI
a fine song in a rose plum atmosphere

XXII
rainbows halo over powder cloud bellows

XXIII
a black rain cloud howls at the stolen moon

XXIV
a gull tries to choke down a wrapped
sandwich

XXV
a comic slug bathing in hot mud

XXVI
flowers run wild around a swamp
blackened still

XXVII
winking sunshine in tranquil folly
on these daffodil days-
we learn to live in a healthy sadness

XXVIII
pearl divers break into a fertility dance
in songs of laughter

XXIX
the places you dream
  the crafts you weave
the passions you keep
  the bitter defeats
the chalk lines run wild
  for all to see

XXX
a poster child in a sweet potato smile

XXXI
the mellow habits of toadstools

XXXII
the live wire kiss of a jellyfish

XXXIII
the world changes as it turns
the moon and the stars in the
black velvet sky always return

XXXIV
gray skies are concealing me
nothing but gray skies do I see

XXXV
honey bees hover over a sweet apple pie
on a leaping yellow morning

XXXVI
rosebud memories dance in the dark

XXXVII
pixies play in an emerald forest beyond
blue sonic dreams
babies in love with the way snap their
fingers for stardust memories

XXXVIII
fly me through the atmosphere and let me
live above the stars - is it true that dreams
only lie within open arms

XXXIX
a boy in a superman shirt plays on
a junked tractor in a sun kissed vineyard

XL
the sun tower traces lost memories

XLI
two girls playing cat and mouse
with my boy toddler in an
antique shop

XLII
a sour protest from a baby boy
strapped in too tight

XLIII
the sad habit of avoiding road kill
on the mourning commute

XLIV
oh he is so cute can I kiss him?
Question: *Where are you girls from?*
Answer: *Portugal*
Response: *Kevin, give kiss!*

XLV
a gentle kiss for a good daughter

XLVI
a baby girl balances on her mothers lap
with her fists full of hair: she then sucks face
and crashes into her maternal bosom

XLVII
the splendid splinter waves me over
for an autograph at Logan airport
I did not want to impose on his recovery
my loss...*sigh*

XLVIII
my beagle has nightmares
he cries forbiddingly

XLIX
bird dung whacks be on the arm
I am engaged in an argument with my girlfriend
one look from me stops her giddy giggle

L
the boy's crooked ills are slaughtering frogs
at the local pond

LI
a girl dressed as a boy bested me in a game of
guess my name

May 2005 - Feb. 2014

Sunflower

(For Ulla Van Daelen)

The seeded paw catches
the solar rays in a
golden halo's floral gaze.

In a world of science
the natural born beauty is
self reliant.

The sun bathers flora glows
from within, it basks in
the art of living.

The sun baked reed, keeled over
from a gnawed out stem, will struggle
to nourish its blooming end.

Heartfelt impressions flow through
a meadows thickened skin.
A lonesome memory nearly ends in

an understated elegance to life's
mortal trends. We can steal away
        the hours.

February 2004

Paper Tiger

The poison pen of a
   jaded poet

The fierceness of laced
   origami

Paper tigers and moon pools
   thorny black rose

A toxic blend of choices
   inviting pain

A silent roar escapes lucent
   tranquility

The rouge reflections of
   the city lights

Paper tigers and moon pools
   invading dreams

March 2004

A Pale Gray Silent Symphony

The red dawn highlights
gilded fragments washed away
in the bellicose tide.

Oceanic sprays hiss on air.
The white noise of a natural chorus
in whispers.

Guarded voices stir up pools
of suspicion in
the art of calamity.

A tubular wave effect forms,
at break point, a clash of the wild.
The gods of war dot the horizon.

The mariner chariots surf in shrill;
swords sing, rawhide rips
the wind:

foils, toils; the centurions of *Mars*.
The break away moon.
The bonfire lunatic.

The oracle of hells kitchen rumbles
bloodthirsty and horrible from
the wasteland of their feudal dens.

No kingdom - no cry!

The luminous coral gates are
the war lord's manifest destiny.
The foam suds run blood red.

The breath of a noble history
dissolves in the fog of war;
exposing, its truths and tragedies.

In the tidal basin,
the waves rake over
a porous sod that breaths;

exposing, the helmets of warrior
ghosts guarding divinity.
In the mist, a pale gray *silent* symphony.

March 2005

Camelot
(for Caroline)

The game, in the body politic, is a cad cycle
of unintended consequences.
The naturalist always confers in stark
      visualizations.

A President's funeral where
the unattended carriage holds
the flag draped coffin of
Camelot; the eternal flame
after a garden of ruin.
I like to see the significance
in a *sea of star fires.*

The terrorist plots his quandary
on a moonless night and strikes
at dawn; baring the news of the
world in black and white.
I am reticent.

The crow's basic instinct is to eat
road kill; after all, it has no inkling
about its next meal. We celebrate
the glade of adventure.
I like to watch children in rapture.

The rouge liaisons of varnished bulls
are a piper for malfeasance.
The buttercups wilt soon after
they're picked and the moth risks

its life for a heat source.
A festival of light pays tribute
to the camp town tales
        of community.
The violet dusk of millennium
is in league with Stonehenge.
I like to break through reticence.

The dog star of a bygone era
howls for a bright new age.
A Pharaohs fantasy in
        the red moon desert,
           after a long walk in the sun.

A quite riot behind the garden gates
and those coarse jeers of the mob
that Rome must have quelled
with bread and circus.
I deal with blind rage too!

And so it falls to you,
        the key holder of Camelot.
I will journey with you beyond the
radio silent horizon.

July 2006

Suburbia

(South Attleboro, MA)

I see powder clouds parade
by big blue skies and feel the
thermal shifts in the air;
I make adjustments for it.

I see the crow returns to
once fertile fields of corn
wondering where the food
stock has gone.

I see honey bees swarm
over the clover blossoms.
I'll never go barefoot
in the grass again.

The neighbors mongrel is
chasing an ice cream truck
again. Why does he teach
every dog that bad habit?

I finger flick firecrackers
in the air and listen to the
perfect echo bounce off
a row of houses.

I dig a foundation for a
bulkhead entry, where I find
a bleached skull of a calve;
most likely,

the result of a still-born birth on
the Tomlinson dairy farm,
covered now, by the sprawl
of suburbia.

The folic sting of an army ant

bites into my shoulder;
the sweat pain is an unbearable
neuralgia.

A flock of grackles fill the air
migrating back to the
nesting area. A wad of bird dung
strikes me on the cheek.

We are infested with
Japanese beetles for which
there appears to be no
natural predator.

Each day,
I bait traps with a hot clove-cinnamon
spice and flame its contents;
and still more, and more beetles

clog our pool filter.
The silver fish are always
hard to catch. I do adore
a good chore.

A crow sits atop his perch and honks
at everything in the lurch.
I don't think that he approves.
I'm not sure that I do.

May 2006

Virgin Islands

(On holiday in 1988)

Narrow byways hug the rolling hills.
The big sky kisses aquamarine shores.
White sands rim around the forest greens.
Wayward goats wander the streets.
The girl with the porcelain earrings
relaxes, draped in pastels.
The perpetual silence among the ruins
of a danish sugar mill, sedates.
The salamanders cleat up against
fungi covered walls.
The loci comforts instinctively.
Across the narrows, the royal virgin
scales the horizon.
The inlets are plentiful and glow
with a mariner phosphorescence.
The dead calm paces the way.
The elegant flora does wither this way.

September 2004

Iceland

(on a business trip in 1992)

The townsfolk of Keflavik had
an affinity for goat heads.
The severed heads formed a
frosty cemetery plot in the
local market. That stew stock was
clearly UN-American but who was I
to say that it's unappetizing.
I settled for a piece of fish instead.

A local school teacher would crawl
under the security fence of a naval
station nearby and read poetry to
the boys billeted there, and with
passionate flare.

I walked along the waterfront of
Grindavek and spotted two blond,
blue eyed, boys fishing in the turb-
ulent surf; they were wearing
Icelandic wool sweaters with the
hospitality of a cozy red cheek.

I had asked them how the fishing
was and they responded with a polite
nod and spoke clearly in English;
"Ò it's really good" and then showed
me their catch of the day, three
silver barbs fresh and lively.

You could smell raw fish guts from
the fish house up the road a ways.
The kind of smell that you can't
escape. I found the cool brisk air
refreshing.

I think I'll go back there someday

to measure the goodwill under big
blue sky parades; a keyhole into
America's frontier days.

The poison pen of a jaded poet
dips his pen in an ink well and
the cantankerous warts wither away.

October 2005

Harvest Moon

(The birthing of a daughter.)

the harvest moon
  in full bloom

a sightly mammoth
  in the starry night

a colossal celestial body
  the gods golden coinage

a phosphorus orb creeps
  the event horizon

a flame-red banquet tint
  the midnight noon

the labored news of
  spit-fired fantasies

a natural born beauty
  a new moon daughter is born

January 2003

Landmarks

Wishful landmarks find
soothing gestures floating past
peppermint wind chimes.

Treasured secrets glow.
We listen to the folk art
of our stories.

Tide pools bubble;
tiny silver barbs cuddle
in the cleansing broth.

Placid lakes reflect
wild wind flower dances
ever so fluent.

The sun chronicles
the never ending cycles
of this sacred land.

Curious landmarks;
panoramic impressions
play misty for me.

September 2004

1968: Today is the Day

I was seven years old when they shot liberty valor in cold blood; MLK was _bad_ enough but when RFK got it, it began to unnerve me. I remember throwing rocks as hard as I could at a picket fence. I watched my target splinter and crack like the skin I was now crawling in. I suppose that I was taking aim at America in a way. I began to wonder what those demons were up to. If I could remove their death masks what would I see? The great American Nero Claudius Caesar Augustus Germanicus?

Who would end a fine song in a rose-plum atmosphere and with bullets no less? In what name did you act? Coward! I remember the boy who asked his dad; "what is wrong with the country?" His father replied, in a broken voice; "I think it's falling apart!" A neighbor then yelled through the fence: "YOU DON'T TELL HIM THAT!" It was a tense time for the kinetics of family; it was a head full of rat poison. It was also the year of the dark side of the moon. We had our first view of it; the tranquility of the moon in full body armor; a view to a kill beyond the radio silent horizon. And the moon rattled like a cue ball scratch in the corner pocket; these are the days that changed America.

We should have listened more carefully to Langston who said one ageless season ago: "let America be America again". If you listen carefully you may hear the mocking bird's sweet song over the clatter of the funeral train. And the days turned glib, but how long until we get it right?

You told me what the culture of love is and I shall never forget it. The merry blend of peppermint candy, wind chimes, and daffodils, in a sun kissed meadow; a daughter balancing barefoot on her father's chest on a Sunday walk in the park. O shine on me sweet sorrow. Why do we skull around in a cemetery filled with broken dreams where the gun smoke still billows in the wind. The kingdom is shocked to relive it once more.

Make fine moxie if you get the chance. The wine soap highlights a sojourn horizon and the loveless may cry blood tears. I cannot hear the voice of reason in this season of our time. Will you help me?

November 2006

Darfur

a distressed pride prays
over lord shadows
sojourn sprites lament
in a sordid duplicity

dreaming through the noise
of a tragic opera in Darfur
a braggart pawn is born
out of the ashes

sand castles form on
desolation peak
gilded fragments form
a mosaic of simplicity

the red devil is in league
with a warrior nation
red light, blue light bleeds
through tomorrow

we wink sunshine in
tranquil folly
we pocket a big easy feeling
no kingdom, no pride

i see sunshine splayed
over a cotton fog in our
mourning glory
what will happen next?

October 2006

A Dry Mist Illusion

The bellicose day strikes
a pose of calamity
in our primrose society.

Consider the mosaic charm
of a pea soup crusted pond
in the living waters of suburbia.

The four winds whistle along
the forest lining and score
a theme song for Americana.

Long shadows sketch scenes
in the plum light of
a thousand sunrises.

The lady or the tiger
is a dangerous game
of blood or honey.

The disintegration of dreams
is laced in the antiseptic ruin
of jade memory;

beyond the world dead
tears in nomadic red.
A symphony is lost in the hustle.

A crow harks a warning;
his bloody beak spits;
OUT, I SAY!

The mandarin sun haloed
over powder cloud bellows.
What mystery in spitfire illusion.

In Bloom County,

the tiger lilies tickle patches
of goldenrod thistle.

The idle wild signature
of ivy covered walls:
nimble sticks in aquatics.

A spiritual parlor stands
in the foreboding mist.
Night falls on

the skeleton coast
dealing naked homicides
in a market of ruin.

Centuries of humanity
is buried in ash;
ashes, ashes we all fall down.

The dead calm
    <will distort>
        a dry mist illusion.

January 2008

Haiku Corner

(June 2003 – August 2004)

Swan
O' elegant swan
why do you wander around
like a lonesome clown

Pond
a tranquil silence;
a bed of water lilies
a lone loon wallows

Rose
a crimson rose bud
sprouts through its leafy green coat
to light up the scene

Mole Hill
a little hillock,
with spiraling scatter tracks
difficult to see

Pheasant
a pheasant shot dead;
the bird prepared to be served,
plucked, seasoned and baked

Firefly
natures sparklers
zig-zag around the camp site
sending messages

Twister
the funnel of doom
a finger of god scoring
places marked for death

Chebeague Islands
where big meets little;
islands joined by a sand bar
around dead low tide

Clams
hidden at low tide
crustaceans exposed by holes
brewing in the sand

> **Echo Lake**
> sounds reverberate
> off the surface of the lake,
> played back perfectly

Sea Lion
a lost sea lion
jaded, weary to the bone
in a bed of stones

> **Arctic**
> a polar pursuit
> in a season lost in time
> the midnight sun stirs

Pussy Willow
fuzzy navel puffs:
bean-like sprouts blossom forward
flowering the bush

> **The Lock**
> the gated pillbox;
> a hydro-elevator
> to the cities veins

Crimson Tide
a slab of crimson
pulpous waste beached: a wag of
viscous putrid stench

> **Lunar Eclipse**
> a darkness blots out
> the phosphor of the moon: a
> smoky cloud turns cloak

Sow
the pig in a poke
smolders: rotisserie of
flavors simmering

    Rolling Stones
    crystal falls basin
    a rock tumbler shaping spheres
    polished like mirrors

Cliff Island
knotty pine forest
shards of slaty rock break free:
a seaward preserve

    Smuttynose Island
    the slaughter house stood
    on a rock shoal, known as,
    Smuttynose Island

Roses
in sun swept back light
snow white rose stems are placed on
pastel clad tiles

    Acorn
    the black oak's hardened
    seed knocks out a lonesome tune
    on a hot tin roof

Showers
a dark cloudy day
a rain swept flowers curtsy
sets a gloomy course

    Snow Tracks
    tiny foot patterns
    freshly laid in the snowy
    meadows frosty glaze

Sun
a self reliant
burning orb fuels our
world of tomorrow

    Moor
    a barren waste land
    inhospitably fractured:
    haunted proving grounds

Moon Beam
light reflected
on a rippled tide at midnight
sparkles the surface

    Hare
    a hare jacks hard right;
    the shepherd dog is lost in the chase.
    a hare tempted fate

Creek
the rusty water
flows calmly through the pasture,
thirsty cows drink up

    Gobbler
    a gobbler wails
    to identify friend from
    foe in the wiles

Ice
an ice storm freezes
the city walk, the winter
sun sets things aglow

    Fire
    a forest burns
    destroying wild life and
    scaring habitats

Butterfly
a caterpillars
metamorphosis spawns, life
flies freely away

Ants
federated ants
work in concert to provide
for the colony

Lady Slipper
the lady slipper
sprouts in darkness to lighten
the forest sadness.

Coral Reef
glaucous pools at sea
a coral reef bustles with life:
simmering sunsets

Conch
a rhythmic surf;
a glistening spiral shell
buried in the sand

Eagles
eagles call to hunt
a blunt act of self reliance
pierces the silence

Horseshoe Crab
strange happenings are
a foot, as this crab is alarmed
it makes like a stick

Yellow Jackets
the smoldering sod
smokes out the yellow jackets,
the frantic hive dies

Venus
a crescent moon rides
motherly breast of Venus
nurturing the eye

Desert
oceans of fire;
the house of the rising sun
absorbs life to dust

Pearl Diver
pearl divers seeking
the mother of black pearls kiss
the jewel of time

Wind Chimes
wind chimes sing for the
beautiful looser in the
midnight gallery

Thicket
a tangled maze creeps
along the forest edge, a
thorny thicket leaps

Mayflower
misty mayflowers
saddened by the dark shadows
of lonesome pathways

Crystal Basin
crystal falls forged
the base challis of charged
timeless passages

Nightingale
nightingales sing
a song in rapture over
crystal lip river

Sandpiper
sandpipers clatter
along the waters' edge
feeling what matters

Rooster
the rooster clay born
strikes a pose of casualty
feeling nothing

Mahogany Tree
the cinnamon twirl
of the mahogany root
protects coral reef

Cactus
the armored hedge pod
crawls along the desert floor
the thorny reed shakes

Dreams
in a boys' dream
the mandarin sun rises
above the cloud pools

Spruce
a spruce tree wears
a heavy coat of snow
sheltering bunnies

Lilly
moving past a
clad of white lilies, blowing
sun-felt kisses

Sand Devils
the sand devils
freestyle their way across
the desert floor

Owl
the owl spies
snow crystals sparkling
like diamonds

Dump Ducks
big dump ducks bull their
way across the loading docks
scavenging greedily

Mouse
a thirsty mouse
licks the honey ruddy dew
drops off a tea leaf

Ladybug
ladybugs hatching
sweet potato aroma
pasted window sill

Bison
a wave of bison
kick up a moor of dust on
the desolate plains

Black Scowl
the black clouds hover
over big blue sky parades
forming a scowl

Mt. Monadnock
the rocky crown loft
spies lakes shaped like whales in
cresent moons of shale

Chipmunks
red chipmunks snack
on discarded trail mix
in a soft gleam lens

Cloud Castles
cloud castles form on
desolation peak housing
Kerouac's wishes

Cove
a purple lace
curtain backdrops a rocky
cove coaxing wishes

Black Oak
black oak dimensions:
fair lady of the wood strikes
a pose of longing

Moment
the blood memory
moment where rose plumb skies touch
mellow sweet tide pools

Black Squirrel
ruddy dew drops splay
over a black squirrel coat
quick time bathing fast

The End

Made in the USA
Charleston, SC
08 March 2014